SCRAP ART FUN!

40 PROJECTS
Using Junk Drawer Finds

by Tamara JM Peterson
and Ruthie Van Oosbree

CAPSTONE PRESS
a capstone imprint

Table of Contents

INTRODUCTION

With a few simple tools and some imagination, you can turn scrap metal and junk drawer treasures into creative sculptures, uniques decorations, and useful items for your home. Look around for old, unwanted supplies. Then get creative! Transform them into one-of-a-kind pieces of art.

Build an eerie UFO with old sink drain strainers and a CD.

Put together bits and pieces to build metal safari animals.

Turn old kitchen supplies into a mushroom garden or a funky wind chime.

Crafting with discarded junk has never been more fun—or frightening!

BASIC SUPPLIES

metal bits, unwanted stuff, and junk drawer items

cans

pliers, wire cutters, and scissors

glue

paint

SMART JUNK ART

Follow these tips to make your creepy crafts a success!

Get Ready. Find all your materials and supplies. Read through the instructions carefully before starting a project. Cover your work surface to protect it from messes.

Scrap Safely. Ask an adult for help using hot or sharp tools. Never cut metal or use a hammer without adult supervision.

Ask First. They may be called junk drawers, but that doesn't mean everything in them is trash! Before you start crafting, get permission to use any supplies you find.

Keep It Clean. Tidy up after you're done crafting. Put supplies back where you found them. Clean up your workspace.

SOURCING SCRAPS

Finding the perfect junk for your project can be tricky. But don't rush to the store to buy supplies! Here are some ways to find cool materials for your scrap art projects.

Look in the recycling bin and junk drawer first. Ask an adult for suggestions of other places you could look. You might even ask friends and neighbors if they have things you could use.

Find alternatives. Most materials used in this book can be substituted with something else. If you're missing something, ask yourself what items you do have that could work instead.

Be on the lookout. Plan your crafts in advance. Then keep an eye out for items that could work for the project and collect them over time. You may be surprised at the useful bits and pieces you save that otherwise would have been thrown out!

Seek advice. Ask a friend or family member for ideas. They may think of substitutes for items you need. Don't be afraid to think outside the box—or the junk drawer!

If you decide you need to purchase supplies, start at a thrift store or surplus store. One person's trash may just be your scrap art treasure!

JUNK ART INSPIRATION

Junk art is a type of found art. Found art artists use everyday items to create art, such as sculptures or collages. Junk art artists do the same thing, but they focus on unwanted or discarded items. Artists have been creating found and junk art for more than a century. Get inspired by some cool pieces of junk art!

English sculptor Ptolemy Elrington made this dragonfly out of an old shopping cart.

German sculptor HA Schult is known for his trash people. His work is meant to remind people of the problems with waste in society.

Korean sculptor Ji Yong-Ho sculpts with recycled tires.

American artist Angela Haseltine Pozzi uses garbage that washes ashore to create large sculptures.

CREEPY CREATURES

Monster Attack

The scariest monsters have sharp teeth and a ferocious roar. Use cans, paper clips, and metal bits to craft a creepy monster!

MATERIALS

metal bits, such as nails, washers, springs, paper clips, and small brackets

glue

2 small metal cans

clay

junk drawer items, such as jewels and duct tape

paint and paintbrushes

pliers

1. Glue nails together to make a row of sharp teeth.

2. Squeeze one can until the opening forms the shape of a spooky mouth.

3. Glue the teeth to the edge of the mouth. Add washers for eyes.

4. Add more features to the monster's face. Use a spring for the nose. Clay and jewels could be eyeballs.

5. Decorate the other can with duct tape or paint. Turn the can upside down. This is the monster's body.

6. Form a ball of clay to be the neck. Use it to attach the head to the body.

7. Use two straightened paper clips to make arms. Hold the middle of a paper clip with pliers. Bend the paper clip over both sides of the pliers. Twist the ends together. Repeat with the other paper clip. Stick the twisted ends into the monster's neck.

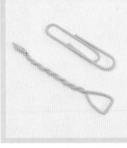

8. Glue feet and eyebrows onto your monster. Paint its teeth or add other decorations to make it scarier!

Stranger Sculptures

Reimagine junk drawer goodies as faceless strangers! Gather pieces of all shapes and sizes. Think up creative and creepy ways to use them in your sculptures.

MATERIALS

metal bits, such as nuts and bolts, keys, wing nuts, and a whistle

metal tins and baking molds

glue

junk drawer items, such as a bouncy ball and yarn

1. Screw nuts onto the ends of two bolts to make larger flat surfaces for gluing.

2. Glue the bolts to the edge of a tin or inside a baking mold to form legs. Make sure that the tin or mold can stand on the bolts before continuing.

3. Glue a tin to the baking mold for the body. Glue long metal bits to the sides of the tin for arms.

4. Glue something such as a ball or whistle to the top of the tin for the head.

5. Glue on other elements, such as a wing-nut hat or yarn hair.

6. Craft more creepy strangers with additional junk drawer items!

Junk Art Tip

Try using dominoes or other flat, rectangular pieces instead of tins!

Paintbrush Poltergeist

Transform an old paintbrush into a frightening poltergeist! All you need are some simple metal bits and art supplies to turn the ordinary scary.

MATERIALS

junk drawer items, such as tassels and an old chain necklace

old paintbrush

glue

metal bits, such as wire, keys, and springs

fake fur

scissors

pliers

glitter glue

1. Choose a junk drawer item that has holes that could be the poltergeist's eyes. Glue it to one side of the paintbrush.

2. Glue a tassel between the eyes for the nose. Add a bent piece of wire for the mouth.

3. Cut thin pieces of fake fur. Glue two pieces above the eyes for eyebrows. Add a long, skinny piece under the mouth for a beard.

4. Use pliers to open links from an old necklace. Attach the links to keys to make earrings. Glue the keys to the back of the paintbrush so they stick out on each side like ears.

5. Add finishing touches. Glue springs along the bottoms of the eyebrows. Fill the eyes with glitter glue. Let it dry.

6. Carry your paintbrush poltergeist sticking out of a pocket to freak out your friends!

Junk Art Tip

This is a perfect craft to make if you have any brushes that are too worn to paint with.

Ferocious Dinosaurs

Unneeded tools don't have to just sit and rust.
Give old wrenches new life by turning them
into terrifying T. rexes!

MATERIALS

pliers

metal straws

old wrenches

paint and paintbrush

metal bits, such as wire, keys, bolts, and nuts

wire cutters

glue

1. Use pliers to bend a straw in half. Make a small flat area at the bend where it will fit over the wrench.

2. Use pliers to bend the ends of the straw to make feet. Make sure the feet can rest flat on a surface.

3. Paint the wrench, straw, and metal bits. Let the paint dry.

4. Put the bent straw over a wrench. Wrap wire around the straw and wrench to hold them together. Glue keys or other flat items to the feet to help the figure balance.

5. Glue bolts or other metal bits to the sides of the wrench for arms.

6. Glue on nuts or other metal bits for eyes.

7. Repeat steps 1 through 6 to make more ferocious dinosaurs!

Junk Art Tip

Look for small metal bits or other tiny junk drawer items that would make good T. rex teeth!

Spooky Spider

Scare your friends and family with this monstrous spider. Cover it with eyeballs for extra heebie-jeebies!

MATERIALS

short metal can

hammer and nail

metal bits, such as nuts, springs, and screws

paint and paintbrush

junk drawer items, such as googly eyes, pom-poms, and feathers

glue

3. Screw a leg into each hole.

4. Paint the spider. Let the paint dry.

5. Glue items to the can to bring your spider to life. Try googly eyes, pom-poms, or even feathers!

1. Use a nail and hammer to make eight holes in the can near the open end. Make the holes in two rows of four across from each other.

2. Put nuts, springs, and other metal bits on eight long screws. These will be the spider's legs.

Junk Art Tip

If you don't have a short metal can, you could use a spray can lid for the spider's body.

Bobbling Alien

Use cans and a cork to create a wobbling, bobbling alien. Add cool features, such as eyes and antennae made of wire and metal bits!

MATERIALS

cork

2 metal cans of different sizes

paint and paintbrush

colored tape

newspaper

glue

clear plastic cup with an opening about as big as the larger can's opening

metal bits, such as wire, nuts, washers, bells, and springs

wire cutters

craft knife

1. Paint the cork and the smaller can. Let the paint dry.

2. Decorate the larger can with colored tape.

3. Fill the larger can with crumpled newspaper. Glue the cork to the newspaper. Make sure the cork sticks out above the rim of the can. This is the alien's brain.

4. Stick two pieces of wire into the cork.

5. Use the craft knife to cut a small hole in the bottom of the clear plastic cup. Thread the ends of the wires through the hole.

6. Glue the rim of the cup to the rim of the larger can.

7. Glue metal bits to the outside of the cup for eyes. Wrap the ends of the wires around other metal bits.

8. Glue on springs for arms. Glue springs between the two cans.

9. Display your alien where you can see it bobble away!

Creepy Crawlies

Fill your home with freaky bug-like creatures shaped out of old silverware. Feathers, paint, and googly eyes make them vibrant vermin!

MATERIALS

old forks and spoons
(thin and bendable)

2 pliers

heavy duty metal snips
or bolt cutter

paint and paintbrushes

glue

metal bits, such as
washers and gears

junk drawer items,
such as googly eyes
and feathers

3. Use the metal snips to cut the bowl off the spoon.

4. Paint the outside of the bowl. Let the paint dry. Glue the unpainted side to the fork.

5. Finish decorating your bug! Glue on metal bits and junk drawer items for a creepy look.

6. Repeat steps 1 through 5 to make more creepy crawlies!

1. Hold the fork with one pliers. Use the other pliers to bend the fork into an S shape.

2. Bend the tines down to make the bug's legs. Bend the tips of the tines up to make feet.

Junk Art Tip

If you have access to a shop vise, it could be helpful to hold pieces while you bend or cut them.

Franken-Fiend

Mismatched, broken toys and old metal objects
make for a hair-raising jumble. Creep out friends
and family with this three-headed horror.

MATERIALS

old vegetable steamer or another flat item

metal bits, such as springs, washers, and screws

doll parts

scissors

glue

junk drawer items, such as pins and thumbtacks

an old toy, such as a car

permanent markers

1. Remove the flaps from the vegetable steamer.

2. Turn the steamer over. Put springs and washers over the legs. Glue a doll head to each leg.

3. Style the dolls' hair with scissors and glue. Add screws, pins, and thumbtacks for extra decoration.

4. Add doll arms. Push the ends into the holes or glue them on.

5. Use a car or another old toy as the base for your creepy creature. Try pushing the strainer's post through the top. Or attach the post with glue.

6. For extra creepiness, decorate the dolls' faces with permanent markers!

Junk Art Tip

The flaps from the vegetable steamer can be repurposed as wings for your franken-fiend.

Unearthly UFO

Stage an alien invasion! A UFO made of sink strainers and an old CD brings creepy aliens to Earth—and inside your home!

MATERIALS

2 old kitchen sink strainers

junk drawer items, such as old CDs or DVDs and pom-poms

glue

metal bits, such as screws, nuts, and wire

wire cutters

1. Remove the basket from one sink strainer.

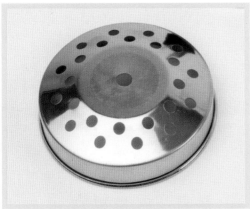

2. Glue the rim of the strainer to the center of the CD. This is the bottom of the UFO.

3. Glue the rim of the other strainer to the other side of the CD. This is the top of the UFO.

4. Find three screws that fit the holes in the bottom of the UFO. Screw them in to make legs. Make sure the UFO can balance on the legs.

5. Make an antenna out of wire and a pom-pom. Attach it to the top of the UFO!

Junk Art Tip

If you don't have any sink strainers, you can find them at hardware stores, dollar stores, or other major retailers.

Tiny UFO Aliens

Every UFO needs pilots, so search through your metal bits for parts to make tiny alien visitors.

MATERIALS

bolts and nuts

paint and paintbrushes

clay

pins

3. Use clay to make eyeballs. Stick one to the top of each bolt.

4. Stick a pin into the top of each eyeball. Let the clay dry.

5. Paint the eyeballs. Let the paint dry.

6. Arrange your UFO and aliens to create a frightening scene!

1. Screw bolts into nuts and stand the bolts upright.

2. Paint the bolts and nuts. Let the paint dry.

Junk Art Tip

Look for small bits at the bottom of your junk drawer to add details to your aliens. For example, an old paper clip could be turned into arms.

Evil Rolling Robot

Turn a soda can into an angry robot on a rampage. Use your imagination and bits and pieces to make the scariest features!

MATERIALS

2 jar lids

scrap wood

hammer and nail

empty aluminum can

metal rod or wooden dowel about twice as long as the can is wide

metal bits, such as pins, screws, nuts, and springs

marker

pencil

aluminum foil

glue

junk drawer items, such as corks, googly eyes, pipe cleaners, and craft foam

scissors

1. Set the lids on a piece of scrap wood. Use a hammer and a large nail to punch a hole in the center of each lid. Make sure the holes are big enough for the metal rod to fit through.

2. Hold one lid against the side of the can so the hole is near the bottom of the can. Make a mark on the can through the hole. Carefully use a pin to poke a hole through the can at the mark. Repeat on the opposite side of the can with the other lid.

3. Use a pencil to make the holes in the can big enough for the rod to fit through.

Project continues on the next page.

4. Push the rod through both holes. It should stick out both sides. This is the robot's axle.

5. Wrap the can in aluminum foil. Glue the foil in place if necessary. This is the robot's body.

6. Use scissors to cut four slices of cork. Poke a hole through the center of each slice with a nail.

7. Push a piece of cork onto the rod on each side of the aluminum can.

8. Put a jar lid on each side of the rod. Push the lids up against the cork pieces.

9. Push the remaining pieces of cork onto each end of the rod. Push them up against the lids.

10. Attach wingnuts or other metal pieces to the head end of two long screws. Use glue if necessary. These are the robot's arms.

11. Use a pin to poke holes in the body where you want the arms to go. Screw an arm into each hole.

12. Glue springs to the top of the body. Glue googly eyes to the springs.

13. Cut two short pieces of pipe cleaner for eyebrows. Glue them to the googly eyes.

14. Cut a rectangle out of black craft foam for the mouth. Cut jagged teeth out of white craft foam. Glue the mouth and teeth to the body.

15. Your evil rolling robot is ready to menace the neighborhood!

Junk Art Tip

When hammering a nail through something to make a hole in it, be sure to set the item on scrap wood. This will keep you from making holes in your work surface.

CUTE CRITTERS

Critter Collage

Paint a hodgepodge of metal bits and tiny treasures. Then use them to create a scrappy collage of your favorite animal!

MATERIALS

paper

pencil

markers

metal bits, such as washers, gears, screws, nails, and nuts

junk drawer items, such as buttons and coins

paint and paintbrush

school glue

1. Use a pencil to draw your favorite animal on a sheet of paper. Color the animal with markers.

2. Arrange metal bits and junk drawer items on your drawing to decide where they should go.

3. Paint the pieces. Use different colors based on where the pieces will be placed on the critter. Let the paint dry.

4. Brush glue on a small area of the drawing. Place the metal bits for that area on the glue.

5. Continue gluing on metal bits one area at a time until the animal is filled in. Your critter collage is complete!

Junk Art Tip

Make a few different collages that center on a theme, like farm animals or Arctic critters. You might choose different types of metal bits for each animal to make them unique!

Aluminum
Forest Friends

Upcycle empty soda or food cans into some friendly forest critters.

MATERIALS

soda or food cans

duct tape or paint and paintbrush

junk drawer items, such as a golf ball, bottle caps, and beads

unwanted stuff, such as an old sink faucet handle, damaged cords, and a vegetable steamer

hot glue gun

metal bits, such as hex nuts and wire

googly eyes

wire cutters

wire

1. Use duct tape or paint to make one can the color of a forest animal.

2. Find something to use for the animal's tail. Glue the tail to the can near the bottom.

3. Use metal bits to make the animal's ears. Glue them to the top of the can.

4. Glue googly eyes to the front of the can.

5. Choose a round metal bit to be the animal's nose.

6. Cut six pieces of wire a few inches long. Glue one end of each wire to the nose to form whiskers.

7. Glue the nose and whiskers to the can beneath the eyes. Add any other features or details to complete the animal.

8. Repeat steps 1 through 7 to make more can critters.

9. Display your delightful group of forest friends!

Prickly Hedgehogs

Put unused nails and pins to good use as quills and facial features for an adorable collection of hedgehogs!

MATERIALS

floral foam or other spongy material

craft knife

metal bits, such as pins, nails, screws, and brads

4. Push a metal bit into the point of the face for a nose. Add metal bits for eyes.

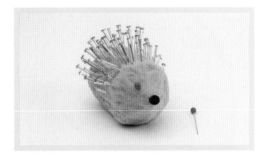

5. Push four nails or screws that are about the same size into the bottom of the block for legs.

1. Cut a small rectangular block of floral foam.

2. Use a craft knife to carefully carve the block into an oval shape. Then carve one end into a slight point. This will be the hedgehog's face.

6. Repeat steps 1 through 5 to build more tiny hedgehogs!

3. Push nails, screws, pins, or other metal bits into the block along the back and sides. These are the hedgehog's quills.

Junk Art Tip

Change the materials you use for facial features to give each hedgehog its own personality.

Wise Waste Owl

Use found objects and recycled cans to turn an old cookie or coffee tin into a wide-eyed owl. You can even store things in it when you're done!

MATERIALS

large tin

2 small cans

hot glue gun

metal bits, such as nuts and washers

craft foam

scissors

pencil

marker

junk drawer items, such as pennies

a long, narrow object, such as an old spark plug

1. Glue the bottoms of two small cans to the tin right below the lid.

2. Glue metal bits inside the cans so they look like eyes.

3. Cut two wings out of craft foam. Draw feathers on the wings in pencil. Then trace over the lines with a marker.

4. Glue the wings to the sides of the tin.

5. Glue a row of pennies or other flat metal objects along the bottom of the tin. Glue on another row that overlaps the first row. Continue adding rows of metal pieces until the space below the eyes is covered.

6. Find a long, narrow object that looks like a beak, such as a spark plug. Glue it below the eyes.

7. Set your owl on a perch to keep an eye on things!

Bottle Cap Buddy

Collect metal bottle caps over time. Then reuse them in this fun project. Arrange the bottle caps to make an adorable sloth or another favorite critter!

MATERIALS

unwanted stuff, such as chicken wire or other wire fencing

wire cutters

craft foam sheet

protective gloves

rod

bottle caps

hot glue gun

paint and paintbrush

googly eyes

scissors

1. Use wire cutters to cut a piece of fencing a little larger than the sheet of craft foam.

2. Put on protective gloves in case the fencing has sharp edges. Then wrap one edge of the fencing around the rod.

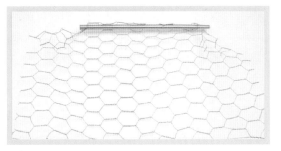

3. Arrange bottle caps on the craft foam in the shape of a sloth hanging from a branch. Glue the bottle caps in place.

4. Glue on another layer or two of bottle caps.

5. Paint the sloth dark brown. Let the paint dry. Add light brown paint to the face. Let the paint dry.

6. Paint stripes where the eyes will go, a nose, and a mouth on the sloth. Glue googly eyes on the stripes. Let the paint dry.

7. Cut out the sloth.

8. Glue the sloth to the fencing.

9. Hang your sloth on a wall to share your adorable recycled art!

Bright Idea Birds

Transform light bulbs into flying feathered friends using metal bits, paint, and fishing line!

MATERIALS

junk drawer items, such as keys

light bulbs

paint and paintbrush

hot glue gun

metal bits, such as brackets and nuts

fishing line or thread

scissors

1. Choose keys or other junk drawer items to be the bird's wings. Paint the light bulb and the wings. Let the paint dry.

2. Glue the wings to the sides of the light bulb.

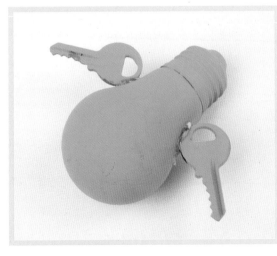

3. Glue metal bits to the base of the light bulb for a beak and eyes.

4. Cut two long pieces of fishing line or thread. Tie the end of one piece around the base of the light bulb. Tie a loop in one end of the other piece. Glue the loop to the top of the light bulb.

5. Repeat steps 1 through 4 to make more birds. Use the fishing line to hang them up so they can soar through the skies!

Junk Art Tip

Try making a standing bird instead. Glue metal bits to the top of the light bulb for legs and feet. Glue a beak and eyes to the side of the bulb's base.

Roly-Poly Pets

With paint and metal bits, you can turn old table tennis balls into bug-eyed beauties!

MATERIALS

old table tennis balls

paint and paintbrush

small nails

pliers (optional)

metal bits, such as screw eyes, screws, and acorn nuts

hot glue gun

googly eyes

junk drawer items, such as paper clips and pins

1. Paint the table tennis balls to look like insect bodies.

2. Push two rows of three small nails into the bottom of each ball for legs. It may help to use pliers to push the nails in. Angle the legs so they hold the balls up.

3. Glue an acorn nut or other metal bit onto the front of each ball for the insects' heads.

4. Attach googly eyes to each head.

5. Push two pins or other junk drawer items into each ball above the head for antennae.

6. Attach additional metal bits to make other features, such as wings or tails. Then display your beautiful bugs!

Sittin' Kitten

This critter may not be a lap cat, but it's the next best thing! Use recyclables and extra hardware to make an adorable kitty with a sweet whiskered face.

MATERIALS

tin can

hammer and nail

metal bits, such as screws, bolts, a U-bolt, nails, nuts, and washers

hot glue gun or epoxy

2 bottle caps

pliers

jar lid

clay or putty (optional)

1. Set the can on its side. Use a hammer and nail to punch a hole near the open end. Use screws to enlarge the hole until the metal bit you are using for the tail can fit through it.

2. Turn the can upside down. Glue two long metal bits vertically to the side of the can opposite the tail hole. These are the front legs. Glue two other long metal bits horizontally near the bottom of the can on each side of the front legs. These are the back legs.

3. Stick the tail into the hole from step 1. Use glue to help hold it in place if needed.

4. Use pliers to press two bottle caps into triangular shapes for ears. Glue them to the edge of the jar lid.

5. Glue two metal bits to the jar lid for eyes.

6. Glue the ends of three small nails to each side of a washer. Glue another washer on top of the nails. Glue the washers to the jar lid for a nose and whiskers.

7. Glue the jar lid to the can. Press clay or putty behind the lid to help hold it up if necessary.

Scrappy Safari

Gather metal nuts and other bits to sculpt this group of tiny animal statuettes. Get creative in finding ways to make your animals' features.

MATERIALS

hex nuts

hot glue gun or epoxy

metal bits, such as wing nuts, springs, and brackets

duct tape

scissors

bolts

junk drawer items, such as a plastic egg and large bead

3. Glue the neck and head to the body. Add a small strip of duct tape for a mane and to help hold the pieces together.

4. Glue two bolts to the bottom of each body hex nut for legs. Make sure they are sturdy and can hold the body upright.

1. To make a giraffe's body, glue two large hex nuts together.

2. Lay the body flat and arrange a row of smaller hex nuts and other metal bits above it to create a neck and head. Glue the pieces together.

Project continues on the next page.

5. To make a cheetah, arrange hex nuts, bolts, and other bits on a flat surface to form the body, neck, and head. Glue the pieces together.

6. Glue four bolts under the body for legs, making sure that they will keep the cheetah upright.

7. Glue on a metal bit for a tail.

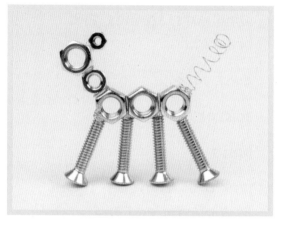

8. Add a strip of patterned duct tape along the back of the cheetah.

9. To make a tortoise, use the smaller half of a plastic egg for the shell. Glue hex nuts to the egg.

10. Glue four brackets or other metal bits inside the egg to make legs that stick out from the shell.

11. Glue a metal bit to the back of the egg for the tortoise's tail.

12. Glue a round piece such as a bead to the front of the shell for the head.

13. Display your safari animals to inspire you to go on adventures!

Junk Art Tip

Add more animals to your safari! Try making an elephant with washers for ears, a rhino with small screws for horns, or a lion with a steel wool mane!

Found Object Fido

This junk drawer doggie is the perfect cute companion.
Use unwanted silverware, a burned-out light bulb, and
a few odds and ends to build a loyal best friend!

MATERIALS

small box

duct tape

light bulb

black paint and paintbrush

junk drawer items, such as large beads

metal bits, such as brackets

hot glue gun

unwanted stuff, such as an old tea ball or old forks

pliers

1. Decorate the box with colored duct tape.

2. Paint the tip of the light bulb's base black. Let the paint dry.

3. Choose two beads or round metal bits for the dog's eyes. Glue them to the light bulb above the base.

4. Take apart a tea ball, or choose other unwanted items to create ears. Glue them to the light bulb behind the eyes.

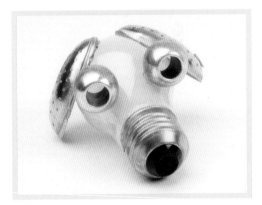

Project continues on the next page.

5. Use pliers to bend the handles of four forks back to nearly right angles. It may help to use two pliers.

6. Use pliers to bend the tines of four forks up to nearly right angles.

7. Glue the forks to the bottom of the box for the dog's legs and paws. Make sure that all four forks face the same direction.

8. Glue the head to the box above the front paws.

9. Glue a bracket or other metal bit to the back of the box for a tail.

10. Stand your dog on its fork paws for display!

Junk Art Tip

Try using other found objects for the dog's body, such as a large can or a tea tin.

NATURE
ART

Hex Nut Honeycomb

Bees make hexagonal honeycombs to store their
honey. Build your own honeycomb and a few
sweet honeybees to crawl on it!

MATERIALS

old metal nuts

paint and paintbrush

hot glue gun

junk drawer items, such as tissue paper

scissors

metal bits, such as short bolts, springs, and wire

wire cutter

1. Paint the metal nuts yellow.

2. When the paint is dry, glue the nuts together side by side. This is the honeycomb.

3. Cut a small square of tissue paper and accordion fold it.

4. Push the tissue paper through the side of a spring.

5. Slide a short bolt through the spring and tighten the spring. Glue it in place if needed.

6. Fluff up the ends of the tissue paper. This is a bee.

7. Cut a piece of wire. Wrap one end around the bee. Bend the other end of the wire. Glue it to the bottom of the honeycomb.

8. Repeat steps 3 through 7 to make more bees and glue them to the honeycomb!

Junk Art Tip

If the spring is wound too tightly to fit the tissue paper through, use pliers to stretch the spring out a bit.

Bits-and-Pieces Bird's Nest

Use wire or old paper clips to craft a bird's nest. Then search through your junk drawer for the perfect items to make eggs and a mama bird.

MATERIALS

metal bits, such as washers and nuts

junk drawer items, such as vegetable steamer pieces, keys, paper clips, or wire

hot glue gun or epoxy

jewel

feathers

paint and paintbrush

2. Glue a key to the bird's head. This is the bird's face and beak.

3. Glue a jewel to the key for the bird's eye. Glue feathers to the bird's body and wings.

4. For the nest, wind old wire or paper clips into a messy circle.

1. Glue two washers together. Then glue vegetable steamer pieces to the washers. This is the bird's head, body, and wings.

5. Paint a few nuts and place them in the nest for eggs.

6. Glue your bird to the edge of the nest.

7. Display your bird's nest to have a little nature indoors!

Twisty Tree

You don't need much to sculpt a delicate, detailed tree! Bend and twist wire to form a tree with beautiful branches. Add junk drawer bits for leaves.

MATERIALS

thin wire

wire cutters

pliers

metal bits, such as a flat, heavy object and a nut

junk drawer items, such as springs and beads

1. Cut about 18 pieces of wire. They can be different lengths. Hold the wires together at one end. Twist them together for several inches starting at the gathered end. This forms the tree's trunk.

2. Slide a spring and a nut onto the trunk. Use a wire to attach the trunk to the heavy object.

3. Bend the ends of the wires to form branches. Place small springs on a few of the branches.

4. Wrap some branches around a long, skinny object to twist the branches into spirals.

5. Wrap the ends of the branches around beads for decoration. You can also add beads to the middle of some branches.

6. Vary how you decorate the branches to make your tree look whimsical!

Junk Art Tip

To add a bead to the middle of a branch, thread the bead onto the branch. Hold the bead where you want it. Wrap the branch around the bead and put the end through the bead. Pull it tight to secure the bead in place.

Treasure Tree

Paint a tree and add leaves with funky metal bits and colorful decorations. Then hang up your tree for all to admire!

MATERIALS

flat piece of wood

paint and paintbrush

metal bits, such as wing nuts and washers

junk drawer items, such as a shower curtain ring and jewels

hot glue gun

3. Glue washers and wing nuts to the tree branches. Glue jewels to the metal bits to add color.

4. Glue a shower curtain ring to the back of the wood. Use the ring to hang your art!

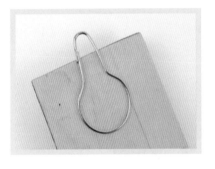

1. Paint the piece of wood a color of your choice. Let the paint dry.

2. Paint a tree on the wood in a contrasting color. Let it dry.

Junk Art Tip

Instead of wing nuts and washers, look for other metal bits that would look good in your tree, such as small gears or thumbtacks. You could even paint them to add color!

Acorn Garland

String a woodsy garland of colorful acorns and creative acorn caps. See if any squirrels are fooled into thinking these acorns are real!

MATERIALS

metal bits, such as acorn nuts

junk drawer items, such as wire, jewelry, and a chain

wire cutters

pliers

marbles

hot glue gun

1. Decide what you are going to use as the acorn cap. If it has a hole in the center, follow steps 2 and 3. If the cap is solid, follow steps 4 and 5.

2. Cut a short piece of sturdy wire. Use pliers to twist one end into a small loop. Twist the other end into a medium-sized loop. Bend this loop and glue it to a marble.

3. Slide the acorn cap over the small wire loop. Glue it in place. Or glue parts from old jewelry or other decorations around the wire.

4. Cut a piece of flexible wire. Bend it in half. Twist the folded end to make a small loop. Wrap the ends around the cap and glue them in place.

5. Glue the cap to a marble.

6. Make more acorns. Then string them on the chain. Hang your acorn garland inside or outside!

Junk Art Tip

If the acorns slide on the chain, use pliers to squeeze the loops to hold them in place.

Metallic Mushrooms

Mushrooms come in many shapes, sizes, and colors. Make a unique garden of mushrooms using all sorts of odds and ends!

MATERIALS

tartlet tins

paint and paintbrush

scrap wood

metal bits, such as long screws and small nuts

screwdriver

hot glue gun

2. Twist a screw into the wood for each tin. Make sure the screws are far enough apart that the tins won't bump against each other when they are added.

3. Glue small metal bits onto the bottoms of the tins for decoration.

4. Glue a tin to the top of each screw.

5. Your metal mushroom garden is ready to display!

1. Paint the bottoms of the tins whatever color you want the mushroom caps to be. Paint the scrap wood green.

Junk Art Tip

Try making a larger mushroom. Use a cake pan or gelatin mold for the cap. Glue it on top of a vase or candlestick.

73

Storm Cloud Wind Chime

It's raining scraps! Decorate an old colander to resemble a storm cloud. Hang your junk drawer "rain" to chime in the breeze!

MATERIALS

unwanted metal stuff, such as a colander, silverware, skewers, and jar lids

pliers

junk drawer items, such as wire and beads

hot glue gun

1. Use pliers to bend and twist loops into the ends of the silverware.

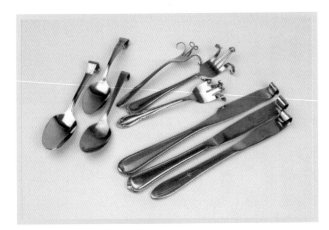

2. Attach one end of a wire to the loop in each piece of silverware. Add beads to the wire if you'd like.

3. Attach the other ends of the wires to an upside down colander.

4. Attach a grilling skewer or thick wire to a hole in the bottom of the colander to make a hanger.

5. Glue jar lids or other round objects to one side of the colander so it looks like a storm cloud.

6. Hang your storm cloud wind chime outside!

Junk Art Tip

Choose silverware that is thin enough to bend easily without breaking.

Prickly Cactus

Push pins have never been as pretty as they are when they become the stars of a prickly cactus.

MATERIALS

junk drawer items, such as a spray paint cap or a small bowl

paint and paintbrush

clay

hot glue gun or school glue

unwanted metal stuff, such as push pins

1. Paint the spray paint cap or small bowl. Let the paint dry. This will be the cactus's planter.

2. Fill the planter with clay.

3. Form a cylinder with more clay. Attach one end of the cylinder to the clay in the planter. This is the body of the cactus.

4. Form two smaller clay cylinders. Attach one end of each to the sides of the body. Bend the small cylinders up. These are the arms of the cactus.

5. While the clay is still soft, paint it green.

6. Roll a few small balls of clay. Flatten them slightly and paint them. Let the paint dry.

7. Glue the balls to the cactus. Arrange them in the shape of flowers.

8. While the clay is still soft, press push pins into the cactus's body and arms for spines. Display your cactus for others to see!

Junk Art Tip

Don't worry if you don't have push pins. Look around for other prickly things, such as thin nails or toothpicks.

Funky Flowers

Hammer pennies into pretty petals! Simple metal bits come together to form this stunning bouquet.

MATERIALS

pennies

scrap wood

pliers

hammer

junk drawer items, such as thick wire and straight pins

parchment paper

hot glue gun or epoxy

metal bits, such as nuts

1. Hold a penny against the scrap wood with pliers. Pound the penny flat with a hammer. Repeat to flatten 10 more pennies.

2. Bend one end of a thick wire into a circle. Bend the middle of the wire into a pointy loop. This is the flower's stem.

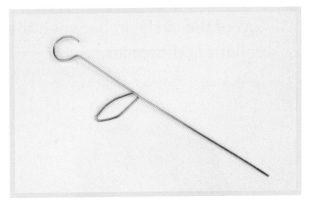

3. Cover your work surface with parchment paper.

4. Set five unflattened pennies on the parchment paper in a circle.

Project continues on the next page.

5. Glue five flattened pennies on top of the circle, in between the unflattened pennies.

6. Glue the wire circle to the circle of pennies. Let the glue dry.

7. Glue six flattened pennies to the wire circle. Make sure they overlap one another slightly.

Junk Art Tip

Out of pennies? Try using keys, bottle caps, washers, or gears for the petals!

8. Glue a nut in the middle of the flower.

9. To add stamens to your flower, put glue in the middle of the nut. Stick a few straight pins into the glue.

10. Repeat steps 1 through 9 to make more flowers.

11. Display your penny bouquet in a can or vase!

Junk Art Tip

If you are making a lot of flowers, vary the sizes and materials to make each flower unique!

Floral Spinner

Build a flower pinwheel out of recyclables.
Display your nature art outside and watch
the flower spin in the wind!

MATERIALS

junk drawer items, such as vegetable steamer pieces and broken jewelry

pliers

paint and paintbrush

metal bits, such as bolts, washers, and locking nuts

unwanted stuff, such as a valve handle and a grill skewer

hot glue gun or epoxy

2. Paint the valve handle. Paint six of the steamer pieces one color for the petals. Paint the other two a different color for the leaves. Let the paint dry.

3. Use a bolt, washers, and a locking nut to attach the valve handle to the grill skewer. Make sure the handle can spin freely.

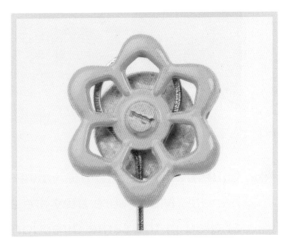

1. Use pliers to bend the short ends of eight steamer pieces with a right twisting motion. These will be the petals and leaves of the flower.

Junk Art Tip

The flower petals all need to be twisted in the same direction so the wind can push on the petals and spin the flower.

Project continues on the next page.

5. Slide the leaves onto the skewer.

6. Glue the leaves in place.

4. Glue the petals to the valve handle. Make sure they are all angled in the same direction.

7. Add some decorations, such as parts from broken jewelry, if you'd like.

8. Push the end of the skewer into the ground and watch the wind spin the flower!

Junk Art Tip

If you don't have an old vegetable steamer, you can also use spoons or spatulas.

DECOR AND MORE

Cozy Candleholders

Tuck tealights into these scrappy candleholders. They're the perfect way to light up a cozy nook or cast a warm glow over a table!

MATERIALS

short tin cans

colored tape

junk drawer items, such as old chains and a metal ring

school glue

paintbrush

glitter

battery-operated tealights

1. Decorate the outside of the cans with colored tape.

2. Tape the end of a chain to the bottom of each can.

3. Connect the other ends of the chains to a metal ring.

4. Brush the bottom of each tin can with glue. Sprinkle glitter on the glue. Let the glue dry. Then dump out any loose glitter.

5. Hang the cans on the wall using the metal ring.

6. Turn on the tealights and set one in each can. Sit back and watch them sparkle!

Junk Art Tip

Instead of simple chains, look for broken necklaces, especially ones with beads on the chain.

Bowl o' Bits

Gather metal bits that are collecting dust and turn them into a unique and practical work of art. Keep jewelry or trinkets in this eye-catching bowl!

MATERIALS

plastic plate

plastic wrap

container to use as a mold

paper towel

tape

epoxy

metal bits, such as washers

junk drawer items, such as broken jewelry

unwanted stuff, such as a candlestick (optional)

2. Cover the mold with epoxy. Press as many washers as possible into the epoxy.

3. Press an old jewelry chain around the base of the mold. This will form the bowl's rim.

4. Use tape to help hold the pieces in place. Let the epoxy set overnight.

5. Remove the tape. Cover the bowl with epoxy and add more washers. Try not to place them directly over the other washers. Vary the arrangement. Let the epoxy set overnight.

1. Cover the plate with plastic wrap. Cover the mold with a paper towel and then plastic wrap. Use tape to hold the plastic wrap in place. Set the mold upside down on the plate.

6. Remove the bowl from the mold. Peel away the plastic wrap.

7. If you want your bowl to have a stem, glue it to a candlestick!

Rustic Rack

A simple hanger for keys, sweatshirts, bags, and more can help you stay organized. Craft this cool rack with a variety of spare knobs!

MATERIALS

piece of old wood

pencil

ruler

drill (with adult help)

junk drawer items, such as knobs, drawer pulls, and metal rings

screwdriver

3. Screw each of the knobs into the drilled holes on the board.

4. Attach two metal rings or drawer pulls with rings above the knobs. The rings should stick out past the top edge of the wood.

5. Use the rings to hang your rustic rack in a handy spot!

1. Make a mark on the wood where you want to put each knob. Use a ruler to make sure the marks are spaced evenly in a straight line.

2. Have an adult help you drill a hole at each mark.

Junk Art Tip

Look in your junk drawer for flat objects that could go under the knobs to add extra decoration.

Smartphone Speaker

This junk metal speaker lets you listen to music without breaking the bank. Decorate your speaker to reflect your unique style!

MATERIALS

smartphone

cardboard tube

pencil

craft knife

unwanted stuff, such as a metal cone and a metal disc

ruler

colored tape

hot glue gun

metal bits, such as nuts

1. Set the bottom edge of your phone on the tube. Trace around it in pencil. Cut along the lines with a craft knife.

2. Trace the small end of the cone on the tube 1 inch (2.5 cm) below the phone slot. Cut out the circle.

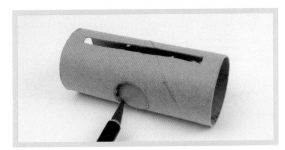

3. Cover the tube with colored tape.

4. Glue the tube to the metal disc so the phone slot faces up. Line the cone up with the hole cut in step 2. Glue the cone in place.

5. Glue nuts or other metal bits around the edges of the cone and tube for decoration.

6. Set your phone in the slot, turn on the music, and have a dance party!

Junk Art Tip

The best pieces can come from items you no longer use. In this case, the cone and the metal disc came from an old solar light.

Cap Coasters

Everyone can use more coasters! These bottle cap coasters protect surfaces and give you a cool spot to place your drink.

MATERIALS

cork sheet

junk drawer items, such as bottle caps

hot glue gun

scissors

3. Cut the cork sheet around the bottle caps.

1. Arrange the bottle caps on the cork sheet. Try different shapes until you find one you like.

4. Repeat steps 1 through 3 to make more coasters. Share them with friends and family!

2. Glue the bottle caps in place.

Junk Art Tip

Try using more bottle caps to make a larger coaster to hold a hot pot or a platter.

Frenzied Frames

Give plain old picture frames a much-needed update
with metal bits! Create a whole set to display your
favorite photos or artwork.

MATERIALS

picture frame

metal bits, such as screws, washers, bolts, and gears

junk drawer items, such as bells and jewels

unwanted stuff, such as a valve handle and drawer pull

hot glue gun or epoxy

photos or artwork

1. Arrange metal bits, junk drawer items, and unwanted stuff on the picture frame. You may need to take old items apart to get the pieces you want. Try different combinations until you like the way the frame looks.

2. Glue each piece onto the frame.

3. Repeat steps 1 and 2 to decorate more frames.

4. Pick out some photos or artwork to display in the frames and hang them up for everyone to see!

Junk Art Tip

Include clusters of small, interesting pieces that stick out past the edge of the frame.

Upcycled Accessory

Make a fashion statement with scrap art! String soda can tabs onto colorful elastic for a unique and stylish bracelet.

MATERIALS

soda can tabs

pliers

metal file

junk drawer items,
such as elastic and a
necklace clasp

scissors

tape

4. String the soda can tabs on the elastic. Try a few different ways of stringing them to decide what looks best. Push the tabs tightly together.

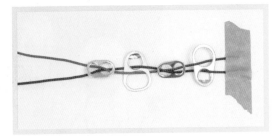

5. Weave more pieces of elastic through the soda can tabs if you'd like.

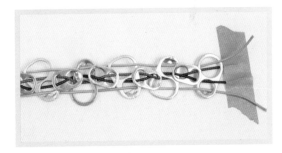

1. Use pliers and a metal file to remove any sharp corners from the soda can tabs.

2. Arrange the tabs in the order you want them to go on the bracelet.

3. Cut two pieces of elastic that can wrap loosely around your wrist with a little extra. Tape the ends to a flat sturdy surface.

6. When you are done adding tabs and elastic, tie the elastic together at each end. Then tie each end to one half of an old necklace clasp. Cut off any extra elastic.

7. Wear your bracelet or give it to a friend or family member!

Locker Chandelier

Glam up your locker with leftover beads or crystals!
String them together and glue them to a jar lid for
a fantastic way to add sparkle to your school life.

MATERIALS

unwanted stuff, such as crystals or beads

junk drawer items, such as metal jump rings, wire, a jar lid, and a magnet

pliers

hot glue gun

1. Arrange the crystals in rows. Make a row for each strand you want to make.

2. Use pliers to attach the crystals in each row together with jump rings or wire.

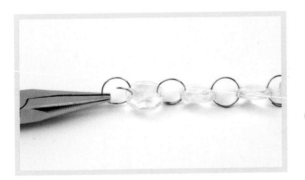

3. Glue the end of each strand inside the edge of the lid. Space the strands evenly around the lid.

4. Glue one longer strand to the middle of the lid.

5. Glue a magnet to the top of the lid.

6. Use the magnet to hang the chandelier in your locker. Enjoy the shiny crystals every time you open your locker!

Sparkling Lampshade

Use wires to craft your own custom lampshade.
Then cover it with metal bits that catch the light!

MATERIALS

unwanted stuff, such as wreath forms, metal stakes, and a lamp base

pliers

electrical tape

metal screen

tin snips

junk drawer items, such as old keys and thin wire

decorative tape

metal bits, such as jump rings

2. Attach one end of three more stakes to the top of the frame. Tape the other ends of the stakes together. You will attach them to the lamp base later.

3. Cut a rectangle out of the metal screen. Make it long and wide enough to cover the entire frame.

4. Use thin wire to attach the screen to the top of the frame and to the vertical stakes.

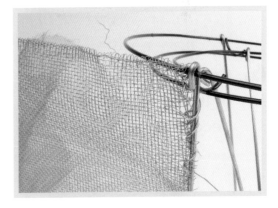

1. Attach three metal stakes between two wreath forms. Space the stakes evenly. Use pliers to bend the ends of the stakes around the forms. This is the lampshade's frame.

Junk Art Tip

If you have an old lampshade, you can use it as a frame. Remove the fabric and put a screen on the frame. Or just attach the keys directly to the lampshade fabric.

Project continues on the next page.

5. Use more thin wire to attach the screen to the bottom of the frame.

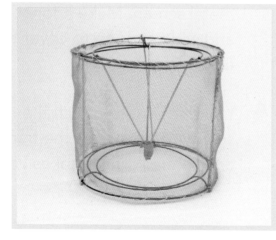

6. Cover the top and bottom of the lampshade with decorative tape.

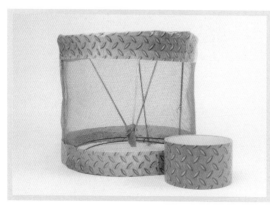

7. Spread the keys out on your work surface. Arrange them in the order you would like to hang them on the shade.

8. Put a key on a jump ring. Attach the jump ring to the screen. Use pliers to close the jump ring.

Junk Art Tip

If you don't have jump rings, you can make rings out of old wire. Wrap the wire a few times around the handle of a wooden spoon. Slide the wire off the handle and cut a straight line along the coil.

9. Repeat step 8 to attach the remaining keys to the screen. Add more decorative tape if you'd like.

10. Remove the tape that is holding the ends of the stakes inside the shade together.

11. Have a helper hold the lampshade over the lamp base. Use electrical tape to attach the ends of the stakes to the top of the lamp base. Be sure to use enough tape to hold the lampshade securely.

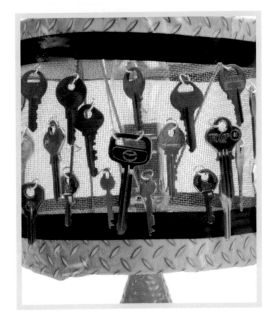

12. Turn on your lamp and watch the old keys sparkle!

Junk Art Tip

Do you need more keys? Try asking the person who cuts keys at a hardware store if they have any extras.

Punchy Planters

Turn simple tins into funky decorative planters with the help of some scrap metal! Bells and fun jewelry add personality and sparkle to your upcycled pots.

MATERIALS

metal tins without lids

paint and paintbrush

colored tape

junk drawer items, such as wire and bells

scrap wood

hammer and nail

metal bits, such as bolts

unwanted stuff, such as old jewelry and wire fencing

coffee filters

dirt

plant

1. Cover any parts of the tin you don't want to show with paint or colored tape.

2. Choose junk drawer items to decorate the tin. Take apart or reassemble the pieces however you would like to use them.

3. Set the tin on its side on scrap wood. Hammer a nail through the tin near the top edge. Remove the nail and turn the tin over. Hammer the nail through the opposite side. You'll attach the planter's hanger through these holes.

Project continues on the next page.

4. Use the hammer and nail to make a hole in the bottom of the tin. This is to let water drain out, and to attach a bell to.

5. Glue the junk drawer pieces to the tin. Add wire fencing or other decorations if you'd like.

6. Add a hanger. You could use a row of links cut from wire fencing or an old necklace. Attach the ends to the holes in the top of the tin.

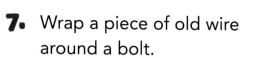

7. Wrap a piece of old wire around a bolt.

Junk Art Tip

If you don't have tins or old jewelry lying around, try your local thrift store. You can often find great junk drawer items for craft projects there.

8. Put the bolt in the tin and thread the wire through the hole in the bottom. Attach a bell or other decoration to the wire.

9. Place a coffee filter in the planter. This will help keep the dirt from draining through the hole in the bottom.

10. Fill the coffee filter with dirt.

11. Add a plant to the dirt.

12. Repeat steps 1 through 11 to make more planters.

13. Hang the planters in a sunny spot. Water the plants lightly every few days. Watch your plants grow!

Dabble Lab is published by Capstone Press, an imprint of Capstone.
1710 Roe Crest Drive, North Mankato, Minnesota 56003
capstonepub.com

Library of Congress Cataloging-in-Publication Data is available on the Library of Congress website.
ISBN: 9781669078562 (paperback)
ISBN: 9781669078579 (eBook PDF)

Summary: Transform old objects, leftover metal scraps, and other odd objects into adorable critters, outdoor art, creepy creatures, and even things you can use! Follow the step-by-step directions, or use the projects as inspiration and use your own objects and imagination to make your own original versions. Clean out that junk drawer and amp up your creativity to make amazing art from scraps!

Image Credits
Capstone: Mighty Media, Inc.: project photos, supplies; Getty Images: iStockphoto: Firuz Mukhtarov, 5 (epoxy), Lebazele, 5 (spray paint), SanerG, 5 (junk drawer, middle), sarahdoow, 5 (junk drawer, bottom), triffitt, 5 (junk drawer, top); Shutterstock Images: artdee2554, 98 (cat & dog), Elena Elisseeva, 79 (wood), Emily Marie Wilson, 7 (tire sculpture), Konstantin Zubarev, 98 (texture in frame), maratr, 7 (trash people), Martina_L, 4 (silverware), Oldnature_picker, 4 (bolts), Pajor Pawel, 7 (dragonfly), SunflowerMomma, 7 (fish), vitec, 5 (cans)

Design Elements
Shutterstock Images: mxbfilms, 32 pixels

Editorial Credits
Editor: Liz Salzmann
Designers: Sarah DeYoung and Tamara JM Peterson

ABOUT THE AUTHORS

Ruthie Van Oosbree

Ruthie is a writer and editor who loves making crafts. In her free time, she enjoys doing word puzzles, reading, and playing the piano. She lives with her husband and three cats in the Twin Cities.

Tamara JM Peterson

Tami grew up tinkering with junk, trying to make something from anything she could dig out of a drawer or out of the woods. Tami lives in Minnesota with her husband, two daughters, and a big orange cat.

Printed and bound in China. 5834